W9-AEG-816

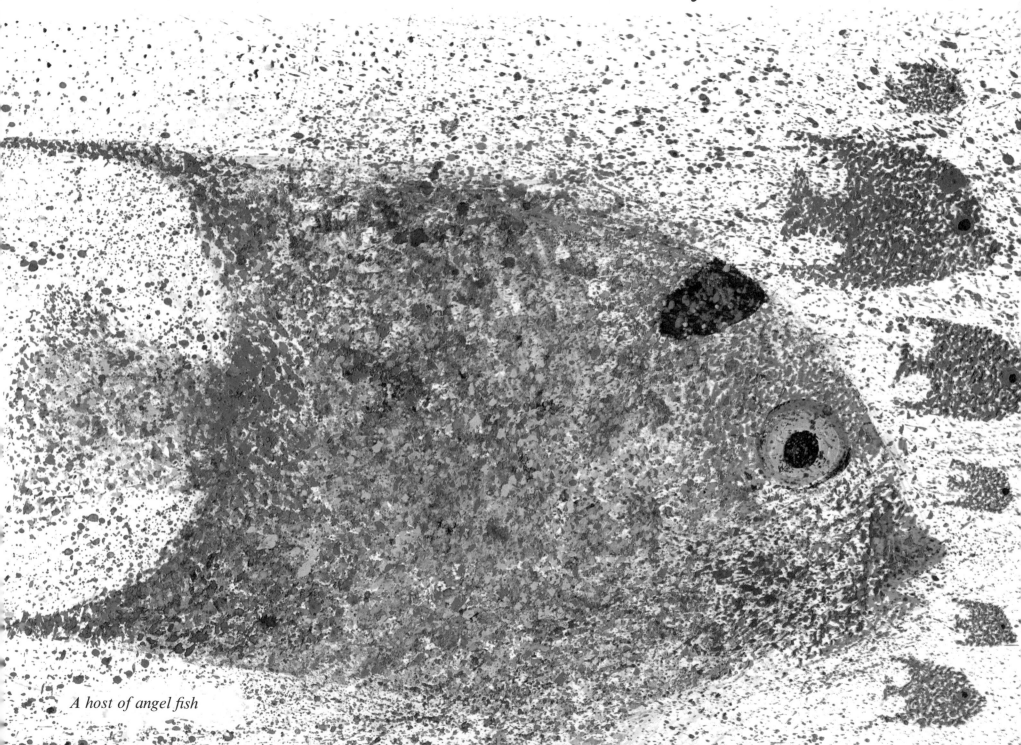

A host of angel fish

For Simon

A shoal of mackerel

Fishes by Brian Wildsmith

OXFORD UNIVERSITY PRESS

A cluster of porcupine fish

A school of butterfly fish

A flock of dolphin

A glide of flying fish

A company of archerfish

A hover of trout

A battery of barracuda

A herd
of sea horses

A party of rainbow fish

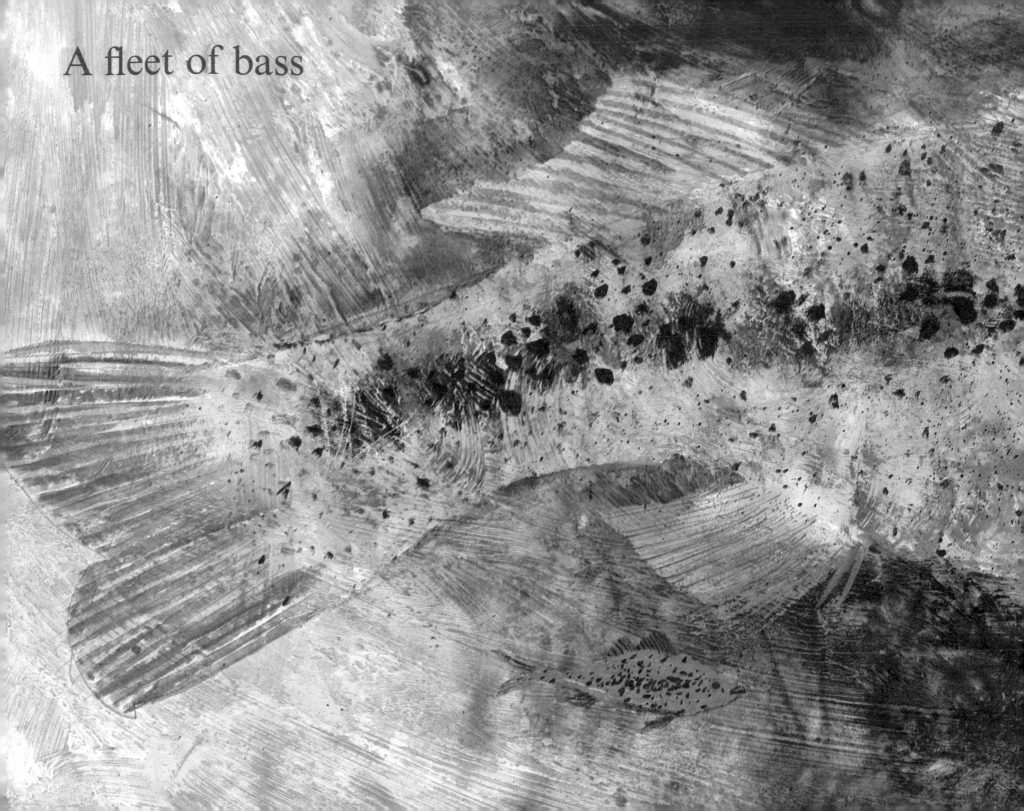

A fleet of bass

A swarm of dragonet fish

A flotilla of swordfish

A spread of sticklebacks

A stream of minnows

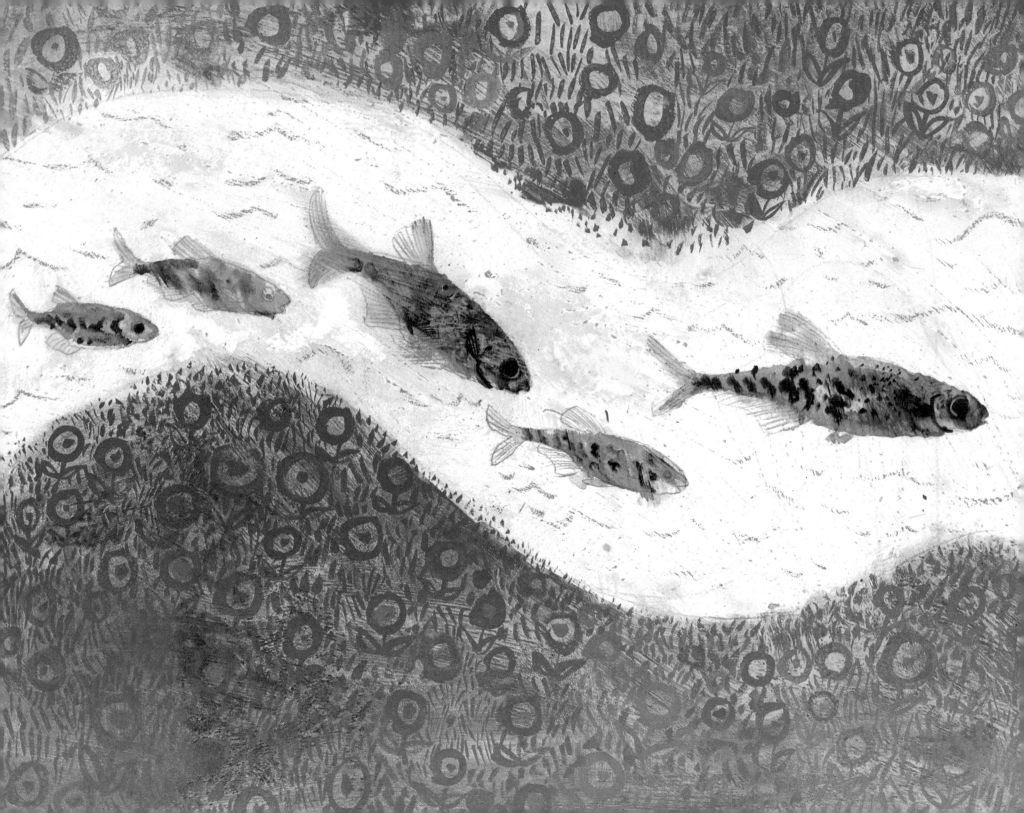

Oxford University Press, Walton Street, Oxford OX2 6DP   Oxford
New York   Toronto   Delhi   Bombay   Calcutta   Madras   Karachi   Petaling Jaya   Singapore
Hong Kong   Tokyo   Nairobi   Dar es Salaam   Cape Town   Melbourne   Auckland
and associated companies in   Berlin   Ibadan

Oxford is a trade mark of Oxford University Press

ISBN 0 19 279639 9 (hardback) © Brain. Wildsmith 1968
Reprinted 1970, 1974, 1984, 1985, 1986, 1989, 1991
ISBN 0 19 272151 8 (paperback) First published 1985
Reprinted 1986, 1989, 1991, 1992

All rights reserved. No part of this publication may be reproduced, stored in a retrieval system,
or transmitted, in any form or any means, electronic, mechanical, photocopying, recording or
otherwise, without the prior permission of Oxford University Press

Reprinted by arrangement with Oxford University Press, Inc.
Printed in USA.

10 9 8 7 6 5 4 3 2 1

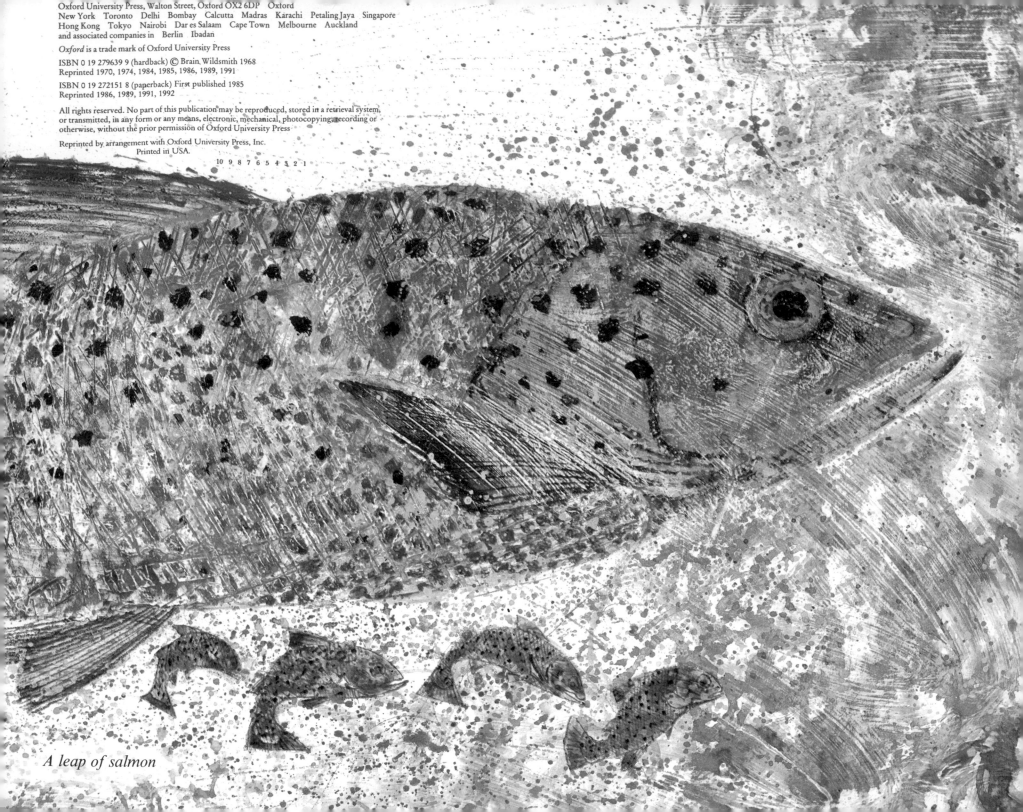

A leap of salmon